ANIMALS NEED FOOD

T0014732

MARLA CONN

Rourke Educational Media
A Division of Carson Dellosa Education

Photo Glossary

bear

bug

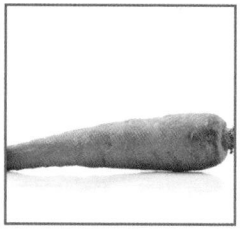

carrot

cow

fish

frog

fruit

grass

nuts

people

rabbit

squirrel

High Frequency Words:

- a
- animals
- eat
- food
- live
- need
- to
- will

Animals need food to live.

A **rabbit** will eat a **carrot.**

Animals need food to live.
bear

A **bear** will eat a **fish.**

Animals need food to live.
frog

A **frog** will eat a **bug**.

Animals need food to live.
grass

A cow will eat grass.
cow

Animals need food to live.
nuts

A **squirrel** will eat **nuts.**

Animals need food to live.
people

People will eat **fruit.**

Activity

1. Go back and read the story with a partner.
2. Discuss the different kinds of food that different animals eat.
3. Why do you think animals need to eat?

> ***Teacher read-aloud:***
> *Food provides our body with nutrients. Nutrients give us energy to be active, to grow, and to keep our bodies healthy. We need nutrients to breathe, to eat, to keep warm, and to heal when we get sick.*

4. Why is it important to eat a healthy diet?
5. Plan a healthy menu for the day. Include breakfast, lunch, dinner, and two snacks. Don't forget water! Share your healthy menu with classmates.